W9-BPO-270

THIS LEARNING TOOL IS
BROUGHT TO YOU BY

GlaxoSmithKline

SCIENCE
IN THE
SUMMER™

Cut, Chop, and Stop

A Book About Wedges

by Michael Dahl   illustrated by Denise Shea

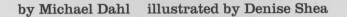

Special thanks to our advisers for their expertise:

Youwen Xu, Professor
Department of Physics and Astronomy
Minnesota State University, Mankato, Minn.

Susan Kesselring, M.A.
Literacy Educator
Rosemount–Apple Valley–Eagan (Minnesota) School District

PICTURE WINDOW BOOKS
Minneapolis, Minnesota

Editor: Jacqueline Wolfe

Designer: Joseph Anderson

Creative Director: Keith Griffin

Editorial Director: Carol Jones

The illustrations in this book were created digitally.

Picture Window Books

151 Good Counsel Drive

P.O. Box 669

Mankato, MN 56002-0669

877-845-8392

www.capstonepub.com

Printed in the United States of America in North Mankato, Minnesota.

062010   005856R

All books published by Picture Window Books
are manufactured with paper containing at least
10 percent post-consumer waste.

Library of Congress Cataloging-in-Publication Data

Dahl, Michael.

Cut, chop, and stop : a book about wedges / by Michael Dahl ; illustrated by
Denise Shea.

p. cm. — (Amazing science)

Includes bibliographical references and index.

ISBN: 978-1-4048-1307-6 (hardcover)

ISBN: 978-1-4048-1907-8 (paperback)

1. Wedges—Juvenile literature. I. Shea, Denise. II. Title. III. Series.

TJ1201.W44D34 2005

621.8'11—dc22   2005024977

Table of Contents

Timber! A huge tree crashes to the forest floor. Was it hit by lightning, cut down by a chainsaw, or pushed over with a bulldozer? What could have been strong enough to cut down such a big tree? A wedge, that's what!

4

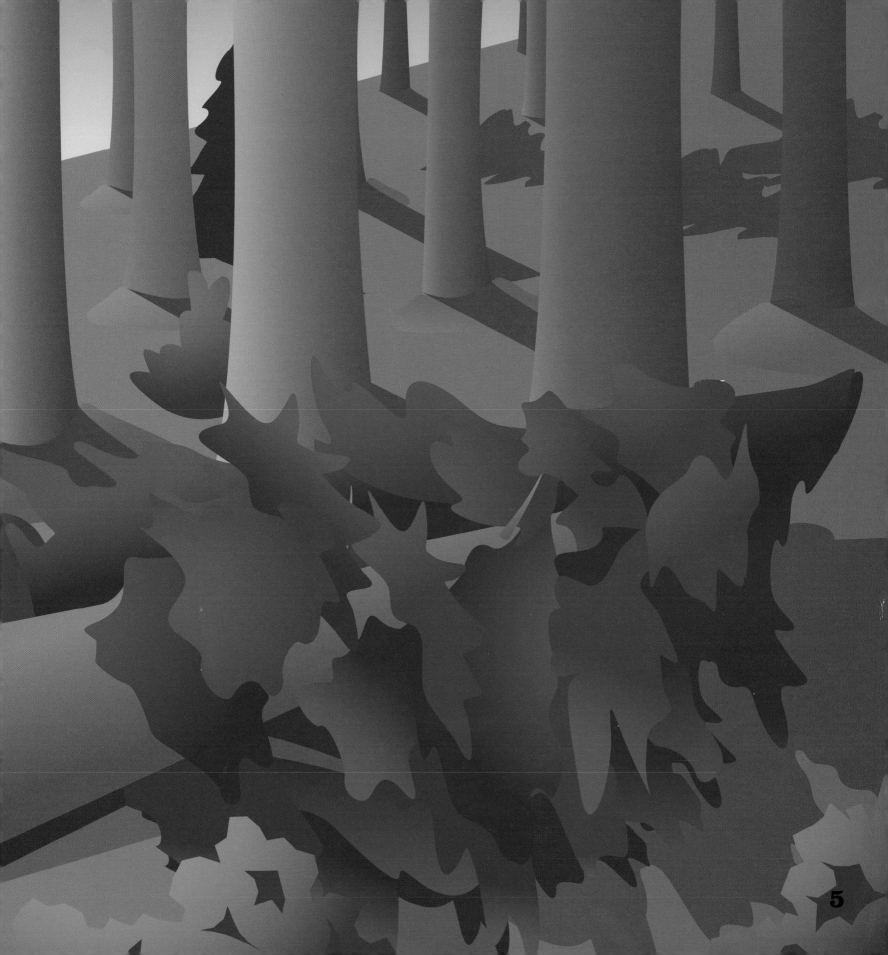

5

What Is a Wedge?

A wedge is a simple machine. A simple machine is anything that helps people do work. Work can mean lifting heavy loads or cutting objects into smaller pieces.

Wedges help people cut, chop, and slice. Wedges hold things together. Wedges split things apart. Wedges help us move easily and smoothly. Wedges make things stand still. Wedges are amazing simple machines.

Iron Wedge

Wedges can be big or small. The front end of a boat or ocean liner is a wedge shape. The sharp edge cuts easily through the heavy waves, helping the ship sail more smoothly.

Chisels

Chisels are a kind of wedge. A chisel is used to scoop, poke, and puncture. As a chisel is struck by a small hammer, it digs and slices into wood, plaster, or stone. Woodworkers use chisels to carve designs into heavy blocks of wood.

10

Sculptors use special stone chisels to shape statues and to carve decorations on buildings.

Flat End, Pointed End

Take a piece of wood. Now, grab a hammer and a nail. Place the sharp end of the nail against the wood. Carefully hit the flat end of the nail, called the head, with the hammer. The nail goes easily into the wood.

The pointed end of the nail is a wedge. A wedge can push or punch through different objects.

Flying Wedges

Airplanes and rockets use wedges to cut through the air. The nose cone on an aircraft is a rounded wedge. A wedge moves easily and smoothly through the air.

Stop

A wedge can make things stop as well as move. It can keep wheels from rolling, or it can fit under a door.

As the object pushes against the slanted edge of the wedge, it also pushes against the floor. The wedge stops the object from moving.

Special Shape

A wedge is a special shape. A wedge has at least one slanted side that comes to a sharp edge. Lots of food comes in the shape of a wedge. A slice of cheese and a piece of cake are shaped like a wedge.

20

Wedges are very helpful simple machines.
And sometimes they are yummy, too!

Get the Point?: See How a Wedge Works

See how a wedge shape can easily punch through objects.

MATERIALS:
- a sharp pencil
- a piece of thick paper
- a couple of telephone books

WHAT YOU DO:
1. Place the two telephone books next to one another, but not touching. Leave about an inch or two between them.
2. Place the paper across the two books.
3. Take the pencil and place the eraser end on the paper.
4. Push! Does the flat end of the eraser easily punch through the paper?
5. Now put the sharp end of the pencil down on the paper.
6. Push! Does the sharp end of the pencil easily punch through the paper?

FOLLOW UP QUESTIONS:

1. Why do you think that one side of the pencil punches through the paper more easily?

2. Do you think the size of the pencil matters?

Fun Facts

An ax is one of the oldest tools in the world. Scientists have found stone axes buried in the ground, left behind by ancient workers. Some of these stone axes are thousands of years old.

Friction is the force that makes one object rub and stick to another object. Doorstops use friction to stick to the floor and not move.

Some wedges have slightly rounded, pointed ends. Nails, pins, and needles are wedges.

Some ships use special wedges to cut through thick sea ice.

Some chisels are also called gouges. To gouge means to dig or scoop out.

Glossary

chisel—a wedge that is used to scoop, poke, and puncture wood, plaster, or stone
simple machine—anything that helps people do work
wedge—a simple machine that has one slanted side that comes to a sharp edge

To Learn More

AT THE LIBRARY

Douglas, Lloyd G. *What Is a Wedge?* New York: Children's Press, 2002.

Fowler, Allan. *Simple Machines.* New York: Children's Press, 2001.

Oxlade, Chris. *Ramps and Wedges.* Chicago: Heinemann, 2003.

ON THE WEB

FactHound offers a safe, fun way to find Internet sites related to this book. All of the sites on FactHound have been researched by our staff.

1. Visit *www.facthound.com*
2. Type in this special code for age-appropriate sites: 1404813071
3. Click on the FETCH IT button. Your trusty FactHound will fetch the best sites for you!

LOOK FOR ALL OF THE BOOKS IN THE AMAZING SCIENCE SERIES:

Air: Outside, Inside, and All Around	1-4048-0248-7	Pull, Lift, and Lower: A Book About Pulleys	1-4048-1305-5
Cut, Chop, and Stop: A Book About Wedges	1-4048-1307-1	Rocks: Hard, Soft, Smooth, and Rough	1-4048-0015-8
Dirt: The Scoop on Soil	1-4048-0012-3	Roll, Slope, and Slide: A Book About Ramps	1-4048-1304-7
Electricity: Bulbs, Batteries, and Sparks	1-4048-0245-2	Scoop, Seesaw, and Raise: A Book About Levers	1-4048-1303-9
Energy: Heat, Light, and Fuel	1-4048-0249-5	Sound: Loud, Soft, High, and Low	1-4048-0016-6
Light: Shadows, Mirrors, and Rainbows	1-4048-0013-1	Temperature: Heating Up and Cooling Down	1-4048-0247-9
Magnets: Pulling Together, Pushing Apart	1-4048-0014-X	Tires, Spokes, and Sprockets: A Book About Wheels	1-4048-1308-X
Matter: See It, Touch It, Taste It, Smell It	1-4048-0246-0	Twist, Dig, and Drill: A Book About Screws	1-4048-1306-3
Motion: Push and Pull, Fast and Slow	1-4048-0250-9	Water: Up, Down, and All Around	1-4048-0017-4